TIMSHEL

~

choice

by Monty Cartwright

Illustrated by Kim Boehler

Portland, Ore.

Book design by Ash Good.
Printed in the United States of America.

ISBN 978-0-9972987-2-7

TIMSHEL

~

choice

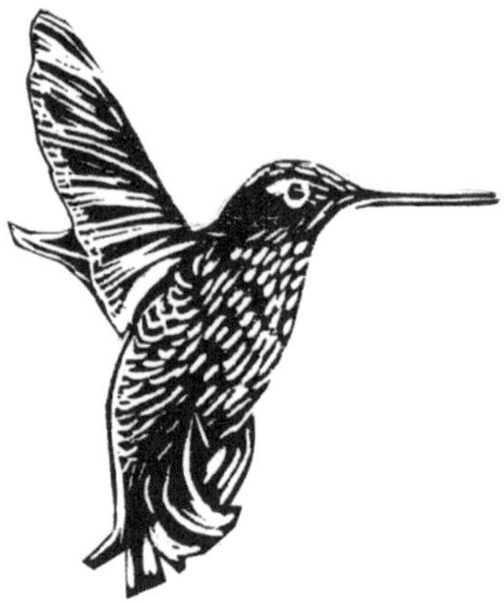

To the Reader ~

The Hebrew word *Timshel—Thou Mayest*—gives one a choice. The word loosely translated reminds us that we can choose our behavior. We can choose between good and evil, right or wrong. We can choose how we live. Timshel has been a beacon for me ever since I discovered it in John Steinbeck's novel, *East of Eden*. It has become the most powerful word of my life.

The hummingbird spirit animal symbolizes enjoyment of life and lightness of being. The hummingbird is my totem, lifting up negativity wherever it creeps in. This totem animal encourages adaptability, tenacity and resiliency while keeping an optimistic outlook. It is a reminder of love.

This book is dedicated to my grandchildren ~

Jem, Mason, Carsten, Jack, Rowan & Micha

INTRODUCTION

I've had a good life. I have no complaints and very few regrets. I've been luckier than most regarding family, relationships and careers. I've experienced and enjoyed a variety of challenges, have won a few and lost a few. I've made many good choices and some not so good and have been fortunate to realize that life revolves around attitude, choice and hope. *Timshel* started some ten years ago. At first, it was a series of thoughts that I jotted down on scraps of paper or in tablets. I would revisit these words at times, refining the meaning of what I wanted to say. In the back of my mind, I knew I wanted to share lessons

I had learned on my life's journey with others, especially my daughters and grandchildren. This project has been in hibernation. With the encouragement of my editor, Dawn Thompson, and the talent of artist Kim Boehler, it is now resurrected. I believe words matter. I hope this small book is a catalyst for self-awareness and thoughtful discourse.

~ Monty Cartwright
October 2017

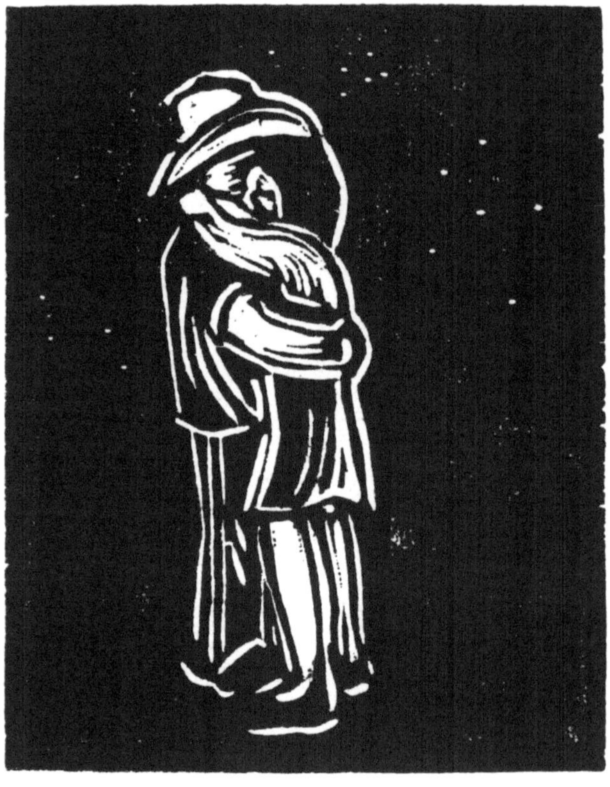

ALONG THE WAY . . .

~ cuddle a sleeping child to your chest

~ hold the hand of an old person

~ don't wear a watch when talking with a friend

~ dance without music with your lover

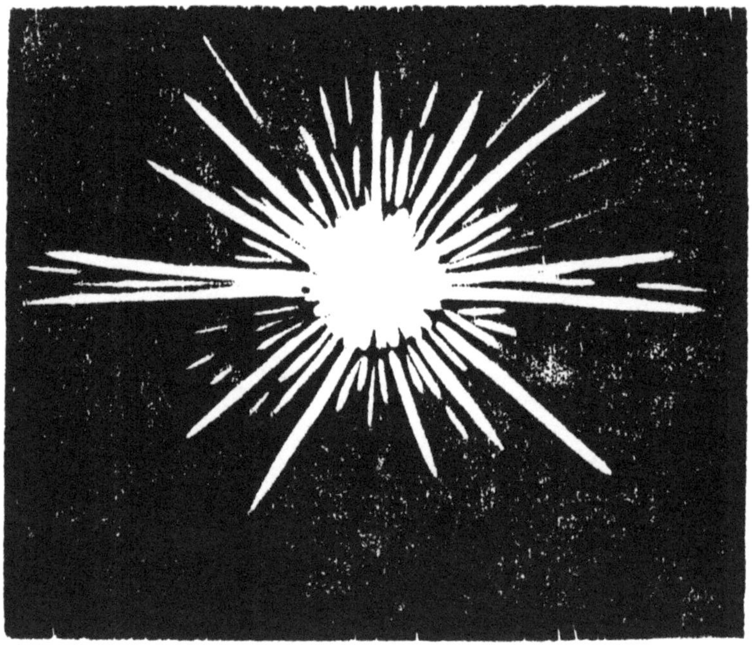

ALONG THE WAY . . .

~ seek people with a twinkle in their eye

~ avoid quarrelsome personalities

~ question those who want to change you

~ proceed slowly with matters of the heart

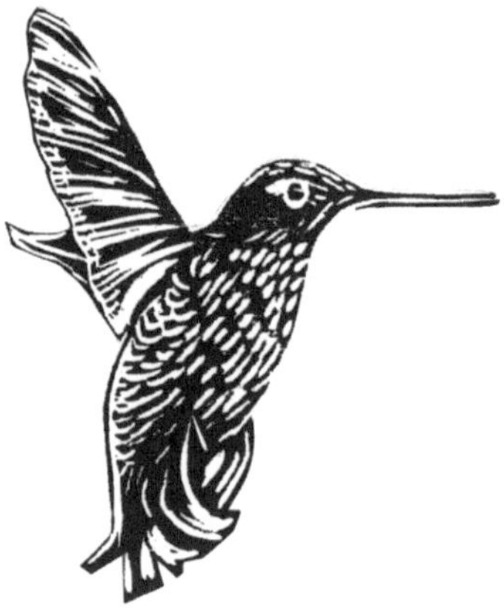

ALONG THE WAY . . .

~ live in the moment but plan for the future

~ avoid debt accumulation

~ be cautious with long-term agreements

~ maintain a healthy suspicion

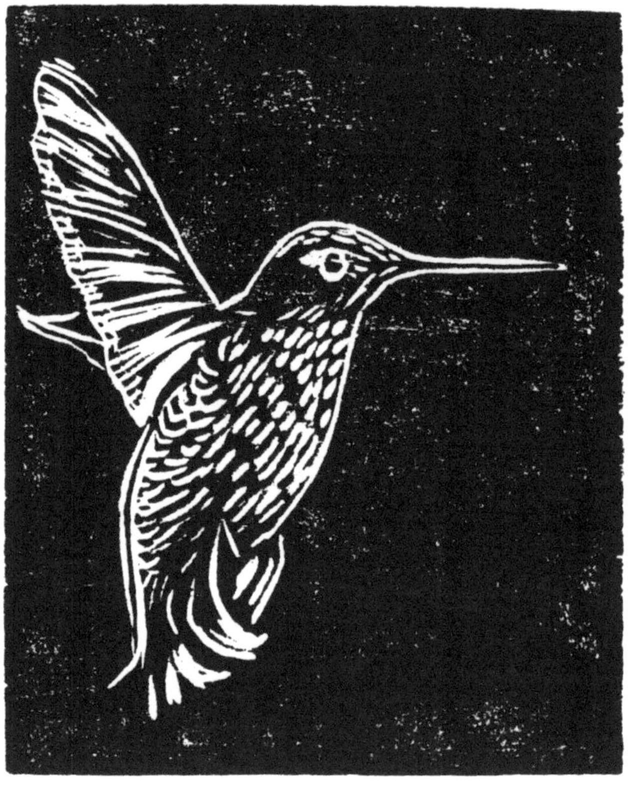

ALONG THE WAY . . .

~ be a listener

~ hold judgments close

~ respect the opinion of others

~ limit complaints

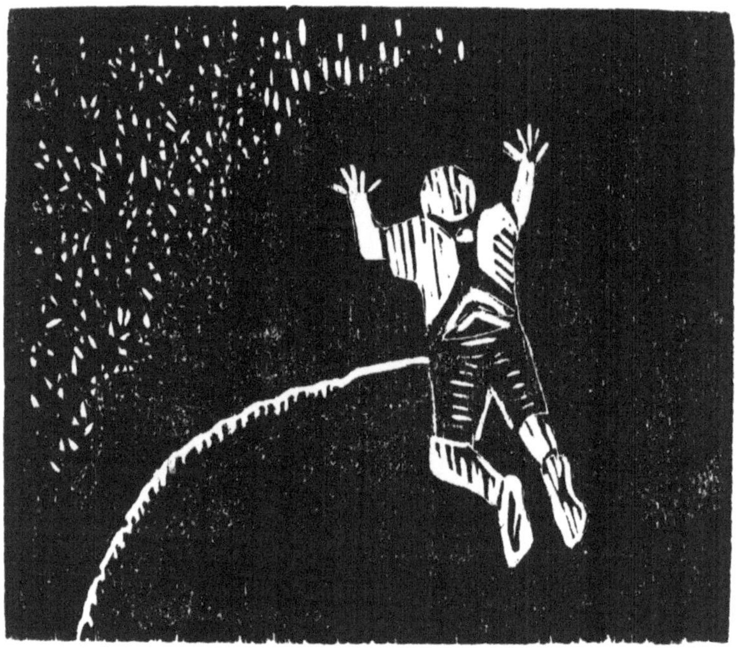

ALONG THE WAY . . .

~ embrace your passion

~ gain satisfaction from work, a living from a job
and know the difference

~ practice common courtesy

~ inhale the present

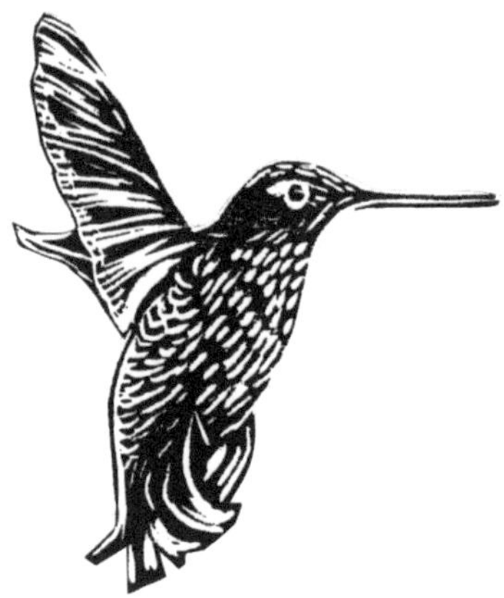

ALONG THE WAY . . .

~ be thirsty for knowledge

~ avoid comfort-zone thinking

~ be aware of bias woven into religious
and political rhetoric

~ question absolutism

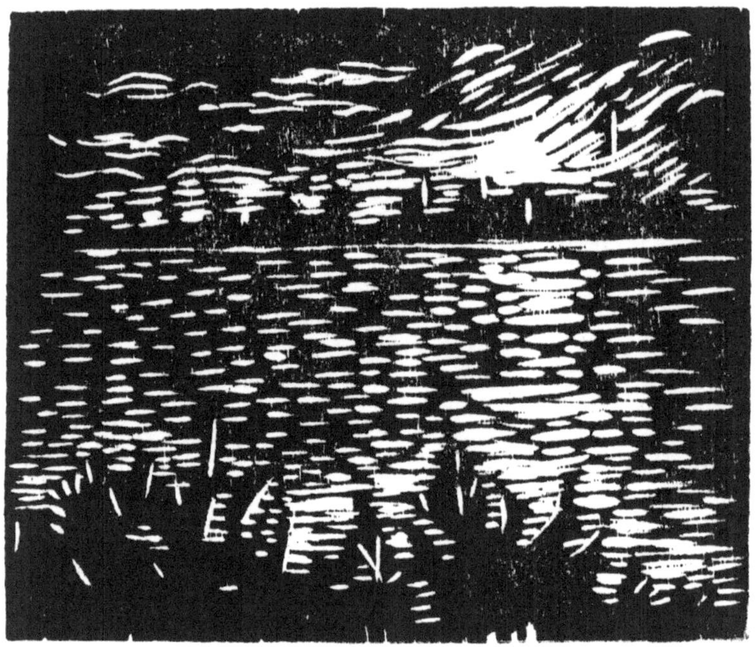

ALONG THE WAY . . .

~ don't be afraid to fail

~ accept circles and waves

~ be a positive steward of the earth

~ know when you know you don't know

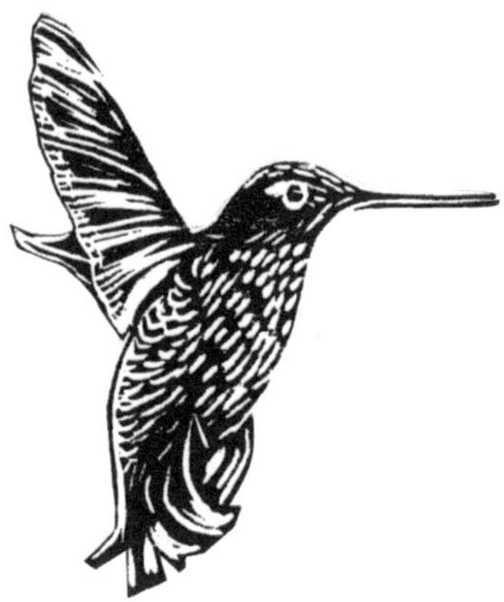

ALONG THE WAY . . .

~ limit rear-view thinking

~ forgive yourself

~ make “thanks” a part of your vocabulary

~ think positive thoughts

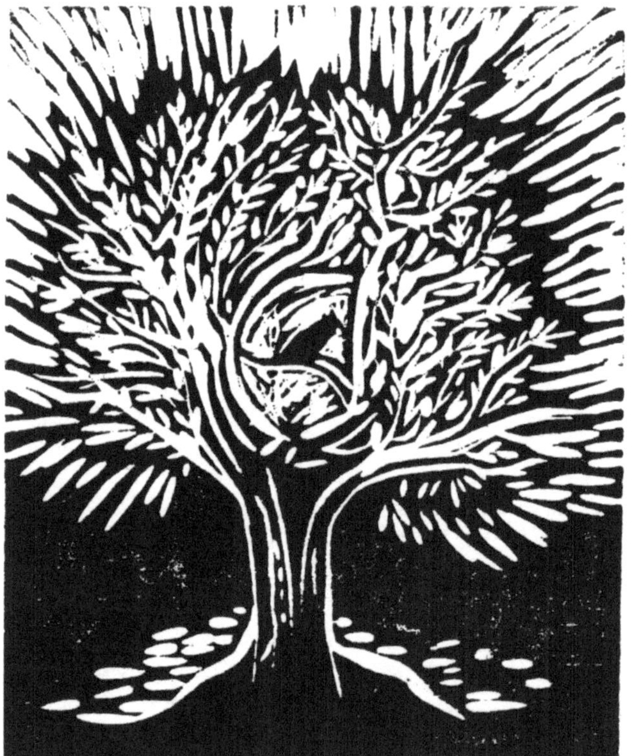

ALONG THE WAY . . .

~ embrace moments of magic

~ realize all is not logical

~ acknowledge Divine Mystery

~ heed your inner voice

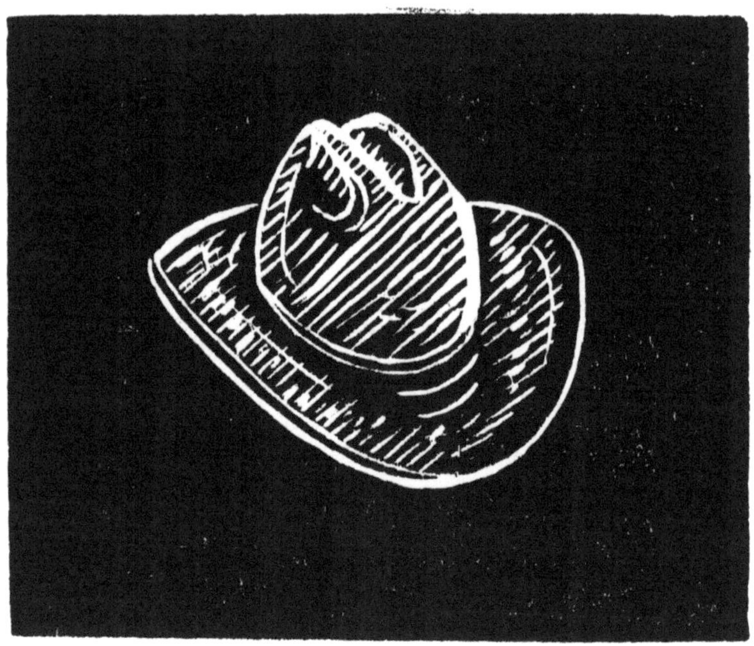

ALONG THE WAY . . .

~ be nice

~ share with others

~ give unexpected gifts

~ do good deeds

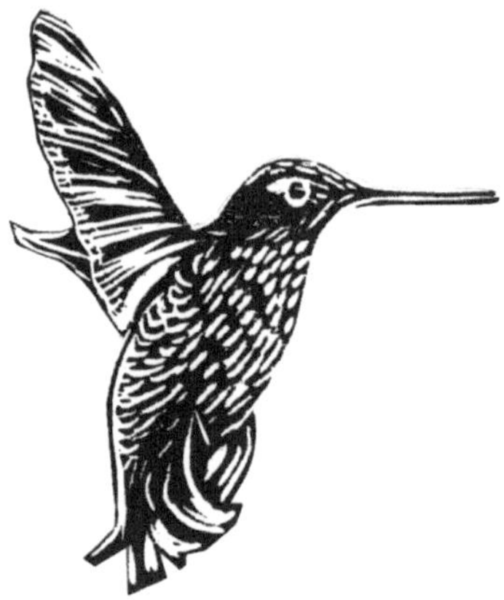

ALONG THE WAY . . .

~ avoid addictions

~ touch the untouchables

~ notice small things

~ laugh often

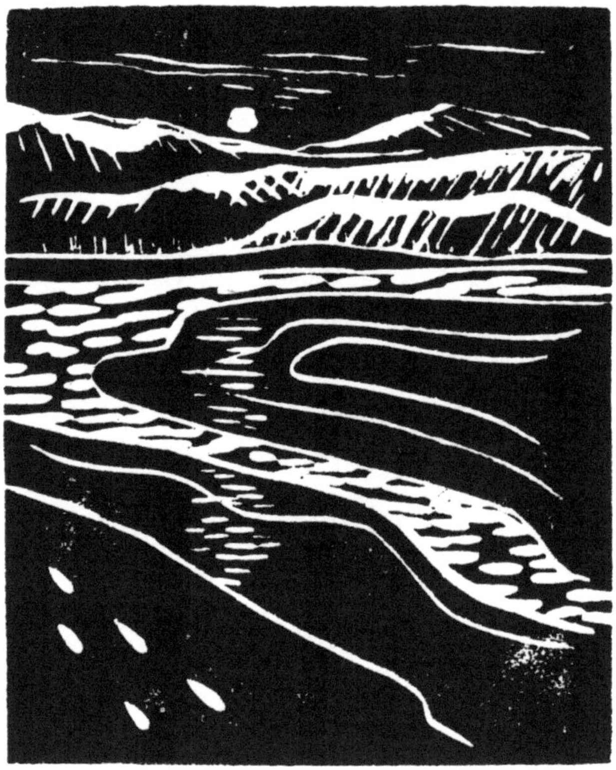

ALONG THE WAY . . .

~ seek solitude

~ strive for simplicity

~ embrace silence

~ breathe in, breathe out, move on

the COWBOY CODE

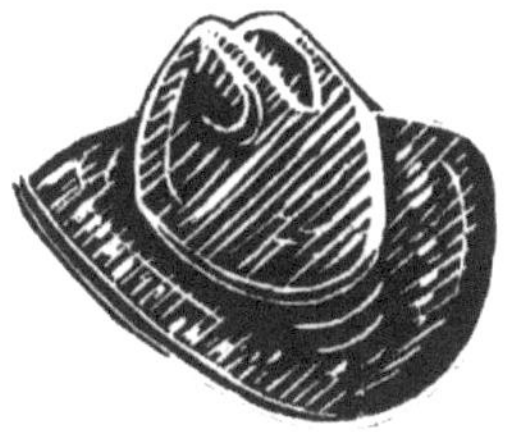

Live each day with courage.
Take pride in your work.
Always finish what you start.
Do what has to be done.
Be tough, but fair.
When you make a promise, keep it.
Talk less, say more.
Remember that some things are not for sale.
Know where to draw the line.

~ *anonymous*

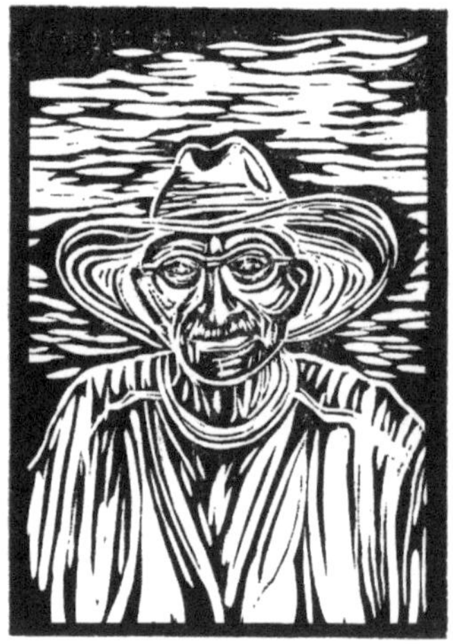

ABOUT THE AUTHOR

Monty Cartwright is an emeritus professor at Southern Oregon University, a published author, Masters Track & Field athlete and cancer survivor. He and his wife, Juliana, live in the John's Landing community of Portland, Oregon. You can visit Monty at www.writingsbymonty.com.

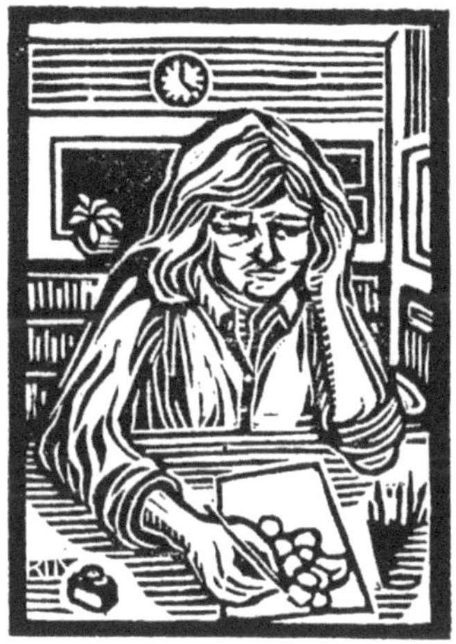

ABOUT THE ILLUSTRATOR

Kim Boehler is retired and active, a former Art Educator and Art Education advocate. From experience, Kim has discovered how creative arts experiences over time can develop into basic equipment for living. Kim adores the Pacific Northwest and feels blessed to be living in Wilsonville, Oregon where she can be close, in heart and space, to her family.

www.ingramcontent.com/pod-product-compliance
Ingram Content Group UK Ltd.
Pitfield, Milton Keynes, MK11 3LW, UK
UKHW061033310726
14089UKWH00010B/216
* 9 7 8 0 9 9 7 2 9 8 7 2 7 *